Barry Hill's most recent book of poems, *Naked Clay: Drawing from Lucian Freud* (Shearsman 2012) was shortlisted for the 2013 Forward Prize. The poems in *Grass Hut Work*, his tenth collection, were written in Japan in the years he was living in Kyoto researching *Peacemongers* (UQP 2014), his most recent prose work. He is the former Poetry Editor of *The Australian*, a Post-Doctoral Fellow from the University of Melbourne, who has been writing full-time since 1975. He has won major national awards for poetry, history and the essay. *Broken Song: TGH Strehlow and Aboriginal Possession* (Knopf 2002) his magnum opus on Australian poetics, won the National Biography Award and the Tasman Pacific Bi-Centennial Prize for History, has been described as 'one of the great Australian books.' He lives by the sea near the Southern Ocean.

Praise for his previous collections includes:

"A masterpiece… the finest realization of painting in poetry as well as poetry in painting I've ever read."
— John Kinsella, on *Naked Clay*, 2012

"When I say that Barry Hill has drawn on all that he has studied to achieve these poems, I'm thinking of the sort of discipline of the spirit that makes possible the lines of the poem, their precise visualization, their music, their handing of space as breath… It takes a lifetime of discipline to produce poems like this."
— David Malouf, on *As We Draw Ourselves*, 2008

"The two 'authors' so connected, so inbricated into each other, the reader is faced with a multi-voiced project entirely wrapped around by the incoming and outgoing songs of birds. An inordinately beautiful hymn to the bird and a union between writer and artist rarely as intimate as this. A miraculous gift of a book."
— Nathaniel Tarn, on *Lines for Birds*, 2011

ALSO BY BARRY HILL

The Schools (1977)
A Rim of Blue: Stories (1978)
Near the Refinery: a novella (1980)
Headlocks and Other Stories (1983)
The Best Picture: a novel (1988)
Raft: Poems 1983–1990 (1990)
Sitting In (1991)
Ghosting William Buckley: a poem (1993)
The Rock: Travelling to Uluru (1997)
The Inland Sea: Poems (2001)
Broken Song: T G H Strehlow and Aboriginal Possession (2002)
The Enduring Rip: A History of Queenscliffe (2004)
The War Sonnets (2007)
Necessity: Poems 1996–2006 (2007)
Four Lines East (2007)
As We Draw Ourselves (2008)
Lines for Birds (2011)
Naked Clay: Drawing from Lucian Freud (2012)
Peacemongers (2014)

Barry Hill

Grass Hut Work

Shearsman Books

First published in the United Kingdom in 2016 by
Shearsman Books
50 Westons Hill Drive
Emersons Green
BRISTOL
BS16 7DF

Shearsman Books Ltd Registered Office
30–31 St. James Place, Mangotsfield, Bristol BS16 9JB
(this address not for correspondence)

www.shearsman.com

ISBN 978-1-84861-475-8

Copyright © Barry Hill, 2016.
The right of Barry Hill to be identified as the author
of this work has been asserted by him in accordance with the
Copyrights, Designs and Patents Act of 1988.
All rights reserved.

ACKNOWLEDGEMENTS
Earlier versions of some poems have appeared in *As We Draw Ourselves*
(Five Islands Press 2008), *Four Lines East* (Whitmore Press 2009),
Arena Magazine, August 2015, *London Review of International Law*, Vol 3
issue 2, 2015. My thanks to the enthusiasm of editors Alison Caddick
at *Arena* and Catriona Drew at LRIL. And gratitude also
for various acts of friendship and love with regard to the
manuscript-in-progress:
Rod Moss, Mike Ladd, Justin Clemens, Ian Johnston,
as well as my son and my wife, Joe Hill and Rose Bygrave.

Contents

1 Turnips in Kyoto
    Bow to the Weatherman   11
    At Shugakuin House   13
    Sex in Japan   23
    Dojo   25
    At the National Gallery   26
    On Getting to Grips with the Heart Sutra   28

2 Crab Meat North
    Ratty Ryōkan Country   35
    Dumb Further North   39
    A Cold Night in Kisakata   40
    Party Train   41
    Leaving Sapporo   42
    Strange Joy   43
    Good News Near Shibetsu   44
    Can't Remember Where I'm Staying Tonight   45
    Wakkanai   46
    On Catching the Ferry to the Snow-capped
            Volcano on the Island of Rishiri   48
    A Morning Walk in a Spasm of Sunshine   49
    Lucid   51
    After Sapporo, Travelling South
            Heading into Kenji Country   52
    That Photograph   53
    Cherry Trees by the Kitakami River   54
    Insomnia in Sendai   55
    Leaving Ise   57

3 Cicadas
    All Over the Body, Hands and Eyes   61
    Unholy   63
    Pillow   64
    Bashō's Sin   67
    Rough Notes   69
    Almost Forgetting   72

Untitled	73
Poor Reason	74
Boy O Boy	75
Like Grass	77
Crazy Iris	78
City of Angels	79
Eyes All the Way Down	81
The White Horse	83
To Speak of Tragedy	85
Lines Found in My Father's Hiroshima Folder	86
Hibakusha	88
The Loveliest Things	90

4 Dōgen's Ashes

Solitary Heron	95
Kite	96
Egret	97
Ritual Sharing	98
Rakushisha	100
Curling into Each Other's Smoke	102
Sodden Thrush	104
Listening Out	105
Debris	107
Lyric Yellow	110
Rain in Kyoto	112
A Son Arrives and Departs	118
Going and Coming	119
Big Root Feast	120
Nothing Gained	121

Notes	124

For

Richard Tanter and Nakao Hajime

Burton Watson and Ko Un

You should not, by clinging to views of humanity or views of heaven, fail to learn about <u>in the fire</u>.
— Zen Master Dogen, *Flowers in the Sky*

1

Turnips in Kyoto

Bow to the Weatherman

Above the last terrace
before the forest
where the track ends

down from Hiei-san —
there's a sunken garden
behind a high wall.

A stream trickles
through to a small
moss stone bridge.

You enter
from the narrow road
near old pines

giving off youth.
You have to stoop
through a rickety gate

to come in under
wide eaves.
One slide of the door

and there's plenty of room
for the abandonment
of shoes.

Your toes. How many toes
can you feel
padding across the mats?

Straw. As if
you've been born
to this refinement

of stable, a native-creature palace.
Relax.
Make your breath papery.

Tune the body
to its whispered
arrival.

Put the radio on.
Fill the kitchen
with storm-news from Sapporo.

Bow to the weatherman.

At Shugakuin House

Darkness in the eight-mat room

As the sun set in the hills over Arashiyama you could hear chanting, probably from the grounds of the Imperial Villa. It comes from another world into this one, yet seems familiar.

That broken field of turnips
white and bluish after slaughter —
tops here, half-bodies there.

You walk up towards the tall bamboo
the sun setting cabbages
alight with silver.

What a mess —
the old ground of your thought
wounds and memories

straw brooms of good intentions
the all-too-familiar earth
the same, same self.

Cold Ears

Moon shadows tonight.
Wild boar in the woods
the deer with them.
No wonder the gardens are fenced.

Did the pigs do the turnips in?
Last night, when it felt like snow
was that a stag
watching over my sleep?

Downtown, the teens in tartan shorts
are watching 007.
It's Saturday night.
Up here not a dog barks.

My ears were cold
after the poetry reading.
Too much listening
to myself.

Over dinner
we talked of other poets.
The first dish steamed of the earth.
That made us feel heaps better.

Under the Carpet

The moon is on its back
or maybe its smooth belly.
It hangs both ways
as fully itself as a sword.
From Shugakuin the city lights
are fat, palatial slugs
aglow in slow time
a gentle carpet —
those civil wars swept under.
No sound. Only a cat
on heat in the tin shed
its natural siren carrying on
as I slope up the hill
past those hacked turnips.

Han Shan on the Bus

On the way back from Daitoku-ji
irked by instructional gardens
I read Han-shan on the bus
agreeing and aging with each word.

Each morning I see a lizard neck.
Each night bones commune with dust.
But still I hope for a pure heart.
The days here give a lucid dusk.

At Shugakuin the hills are a cradle
the moon a half lamp. I came
up by the clinic and school
a short cut through the shrine

in under its bracing gate.
A pine roped behind a red fence.
A bell hanging in the dark.
I was quick around it, then out

up between the frostbitten cabbages
unnameables under black plastic
that dug-field of turnips —
wounded torsos, loose white flesh.

Like the housewife ahead of me
groceries loaded each arm.
Soon I had the climb to myself.
All the craggy hermit said was true.

I reached my gate in the low wall.
Further up, perfectly pruned peach trees
stood spiky under the stars.
For the crystal night I had

a wild piss beside the house
then went inside to forget sutras
drink wine. The rice steams. Truly
I don't know how old I am.

Shallow

The helpful neighbour
who gardens across the way
standing inside the wire
showed you where the boar
dug under the enclosure
and stretched his length
down into his creative work.

Be careful out here
at night, he laughed
pointing to the shallow grave.

Without You

At Daisen-in
behind the raked garden
near the headstones
my face brushed a camellia bush.

Winter buds.
They were younger than you, or me.
The tree might have been
more our age.

Shamelessly, I picked
a bud for the Buddha
in this empty eight-mat room.
There it lolls — stemless

and without water
as I am without you.
Tightly pink, bursting —
my favourite flower.

Returning to Mat

It's twice a day.
At least give
yourself credit for that.

You can't fail
looking into a garden
with a teahouse
and a thrush in leaf-litter.

And even if you
loose the bird
and the dilapidated teahouse
is locked to strangers

you just have to *consume*
more time. Simple.
You don't have to
say simple, or think simple.

Just accept the monkey
on your back. Ok –
roof, monkeys.
You'll know when

you fail, or fail better.
Day by day is good
with the oil boiling
over the blazing fire.

Silver Pavilion

Your poet ... hopes to retire altogether from his humanity and to transmigrate into immortal Phoenix or supernal Swan.
       Harold Stewart, *By the Old Walls of Kyoto*

Phoenix on the ridge-line. The one
beloved of my compatriot
after his encounter with death.
Thinking of him
I took one photo after another
as if it might take off.

Later, downtown
a kite landed on an office block.
I caught it between telegraph poles
all beak and shoulder, unruffled.
You could sense the lice
that keep its sleek company.

Eventually, its wings spread south.
I carried on to the west
bought a ticket to the cinema
the name of the film unknown to me.
Happy moment: it was about dragon-riding.

Walking back to my grass hut
the moon smouldered.
It's what they are calling a warm winter.
The bears won't sleep, they'll stay young.
I have much flying to do tonight.

Confusion

The other morning
as I came into the kitchen
a scrap ahead of my step
flicked up, out of the way.

I took one more step
and it did it again —
then paused for the frog
as gold as an autumn leaf.

Along its head, a thin white stripe.
A vanilla underside
with a green tinge throughout —
a distant memory of spring.

I trapped it in a sake glass
carried it outside
placed it on a moss-bank
under the bamboo, palpitating.

A sign on the cupboard says:
'Please store your food.
A huge weasel (*itachi*) visits.
Really!!!!'

Can a weasel morph
into a frog? I wondered.
Above me, at fiery Hiei-san
many a monk has confused himself.

Sex in Japan

Are you writing the same poem
or just getting older
forgetting the details?

Your journey out
began here:
in a ryōkan in Nikko
fucking your first wife
learning about deceptively hard
mats, love as ritual –
your own paper-thin walls.

From *Hiroshima Mon Amour*
to *In the Realm of the Senses*.
After several wives
you just might know
the extent to which a man
can undo himself.

That was then. Now?
You're back in Kyoto
half remembering the python
a middle-aged tart
looped about her belly and thighs.
Her grinning cavernous show
had a row of Japanese men
leaning forward in unison.

Now it's all girls
(as you were, then
not much more than a boy).
They fill the cartoon mags
like pastel-coloured sweets
a damp patch on each wrapping.
Kawabata, eat your heart out.

I don't understand.
The elderly women are beautiful.
And I can't keep my eyes off those
lacquered reds married to black –
the bowls, the luscious almost nauseatingly
scarlet or vermilion serving trays
and that blood-red teapot
with its long, thin silly spout.

Dojo

The teacher has a scoop of a face, like a sliced melon. He is quick to welcome: a student finds a chair, set, you later realise, under the lustrous poster of the young man who is the teacher's pupil, now the All-Japan Champion delivering a *mawashi-geri* with the ease of a leopard stretching. The sole of his striking foot is soft/hard, and higher than his head. It's a regular class.

No one's perfect in the warm-up.
Every body has cold hamstrings
a groin to care for, fine ankles.

Everyone can count the ten thousand
kicks and punches in their sleep.
Forms dream them.

Forms take them by the flying hand.
Forms marry their dance with respect
with death.

Sweat sweetens intent
and the snap of Sensei's *ghi*.
A monk ties his sleeves back

for the day's chores;
Sensei lets them be
in furious feather of pointedness.

No quincy belly, head straight
the body as balanced as mercury.
Eye to eye, face to face transmission.

The drum in everyone beats.
I am seated, only watching
my heart racing for my youth.

At the National Gallery

Shinto Goddess

She's wood replanted
carved to sit like an upturned root.

You'd offer her onions, clover
maybe one of those turnips.

Say she's 'primitive'.
Go on — say it to your
civilized companions.
You try, but slip into murmuring 'tribal'
a term they don't take to.

She's featureless, almost.
All grain and earth and shadow.
Parts of her seem burnt.

Where have you met before?

Original Face

Just inside the door
of the Room of the Immortals —
    an ancient silver script
        cuts its way under the glass.
Each character as strong, as swift
as a dolphin breaking the surface.

It was beside the Tang Dynasty stone face
I'll hold in my mind tonight
    sinking into slow sleep
        with that play about the mouth —
its all-round music
and oceanic smirk.

On Getting to Grips with the Heart Sutra

Surge plays on and off-key, mainly on. A gurgling wins over words,
                                                                         almost pings
dances down, pocks stone, thrums, flares in little hollows from time,
                                                                          like flames —

You sat by the door with the door closed and the rush was rush enough —
rain arrives and stays, is downpour, it wants the door closed, listen to its fall

as welcome as sleep is welcome, in far reaches of temples, it's touch cool
and still you are dry in the warm room, the rain sheets the glass, it's trying

to wash in, splashes back, onto the stone step, its gush, like your waking,
                                                                           is all there
all of the time now, dimpling and flooding, dimpling and filling the mind —

rain all night and now rain the whole morning, flooding the new morning,
                                                                              making it
the old rain, time-worn, it falls as it always falls, emptying itself as it
                                                                        swells back up

gutters have all the time in the world, fat pebbled, grey stones grey as rain
light falling out of rain as drops, smooth stones, each drop loving stones,
                                                                     wasting themselves

the rain is all love of morning, having fallen all night, creeks, a river
it rushes on past out there, you can see it through the glass, the dark sheets

the morning's light yet to come right in, the rain to wash the day, you
if you'd let it, open your mouth, there's no roof, look up now, look up
                                                                        into the sky…

The sound of rain off wide eaves sooths the mind, the water fall, its force
the force in its gentleness off wide eaves sooths the mind, its outside-inside
                                                                       sounds falling…

It gives vigour, it takes vigour away, it washes the mind.
The force of rain off wide eaves washes the mind.

      Only the eaves, the eaves save the walls. Open the door if you dare!

On its slide, the door sound is avalanche. Fills the mind — with words, war.
What comes close is what you must have been waiting for, but who was
                                                                                              to know.

The ten thousand black horses ride on down from the sky over Hiei-san.
The ten thousand horses fall from their night into morning.

The water roar is grey-toned, silver flecked, black with a flame in it, wild

heavy, each streaming mane lead-heavy, thickening with downpour.

Hooves clatter on the stones, steam from their nostrils shoots into yours.
The clatter, the rumble out there! Its fox trot and stomp, the creature is
                                                                                               to be met.

If a breeze, the rain would whinny, hiss. As it is, there are the drops, the ten
thousand drops into the heart, the sound that beats inside and outside

the rain-sound that makes an eve for the mind (all these words)
the rain-sound that beats on the walls of the mind, eases it, needs

the mind to be inside it outside in the instant, at the same time.

Your welling up, a feeling of tears in the doorway, the heart wishing not
                                                                                   to be hurt by rain
the body's alarm at the force of it all, the heat of its roar, its boiling ice.

Each drop has its outside sound, each drop breaks open from its centre
    a catastrophe of walls crashing in, the empty sound splashing out —

and the running on of that, the spillage and joy of breakage.
    Simple: rain-sound is celebration, of release, nothing more, nothing less.

No. The sound of rain tightens, its swells into itself, seizes its own notes
this way then that in its own race before bursting, there's more than one
                                                  stream

coming down, the light one that breaks — you catch, you think, its notes
and a dark one underneath, its pulse green and of the forest

it pushes the others about, but without reason, it holds some up, lets
                                                  others go
drives their shattering without reason, or without reason that you can grasp,
                                                  the sound

let in through the door your heart open
or as open as can be in a single morning woken by doves in the rain

the whole sound doubled and tripled by the percussive mystery and lack
of melody, or a melody that splatters here and there at your feet, threatening

to wet your socks, give you cold feet! Tempting it is to shut the door
keep the sound at bay, the roaring-cold-fire-sound you can barely fathom.

The door stays open. The sound remains a strangely terrible joyous
                                                  sensation.
It remains what it is, its drum in your throat, in the belly's pith

in the mind's eye, the ear's shell, it's in under the tongue that won't stop
wagging, jigging words on a string out there on the stone pebbles —

language does its dance in lovely runnels receiving rain
words dissolve out there, they wash back into the earth, leaving the sound

unfathomable. You keep sitting there like a voice-hearer —
those old timers who just wanted the lesson, the sutra straight, without rain —

staying you, keeping you here, come to think of it, the one dry thought:
warmth arrives because you are inside it, warmth of the essence

the flow in warmth is the flow of something, as sure as a dove's call
the birds that woke you with their bubbly murmurs, their warm rain sounds.

The warmth's there as it empties itself like notes like drops
inside and outside at once, the sound crossing, re-crossing over —

thus speaking, you can say this, sound summonses the words
washing them in, words born, re-born in the pock of the mouth

and washed down, a body of water, words bound for the blood stream
words washed down incessantly, words for the gullet, vanishing into the
$$\text{runnels} -$$

running off eaves that keep walls of the mind standing
washed off eaves back into earth that mothers rain.

Rain, rain, falling inside its sound — rain-body, joy.
Rain, the rain, falling outside its sound — rain-body, joy.

2

Crab Meat North

Ratty Ryōkan Country

The Island of Sado
Morning and evening I see it in my dreams
Together with the gentle face of my mother.
            Zen Master Ryōkan

1
An icy wind blows off Sado.
They dug for gold
and buried dissenters.

One day I'll go
to see the drummers
whip up the waves.

Here I'm in exile
just looking across
beach ravens ratty as gulls.

At home, it's spring.
I've left a garden of wattlebird
chicks blooming in olive trees —

our crows chased off ferociously.
Ryōkan listened
to the long sounds of geese

ploughing their way over.
Wish I didn't have to think
of loneliness

as often as Ryōkan.
In this cloudy country
during the long snows

he kept finding his way.

2

After Niigata —
paddy fields and white swans
the last of the persimmons
aglow in toy gardens.

Along the embankments
between the stubble
a girl swings her schoolbag
dreaming of Lilly Chu Chu.

In this carriage
the royal blue
of boy's blazers and trousers.
Manly snow-capped mountains inland.

Now the kids have left the train
leaving me alone
as a place name. Izumozaki —
empty as a begging bowl.

I have my back to the sea.
The snowy range will lead me
to his hut up there
in winter in sickness often.

Hey kids, he called
on the good days.
He had a ball tucked
up in a sleeve

even a monk
is allowed
to shed
a tear on.

3

The storm arrived, as the fisherman warned.
Now you can't see Sado.
It's all sashimi and foam.

Behind the breakwater
the wind scallops the sea.
Cormorants bury their heads

make no more progress than a poet.
But I've been taken in
like a mendicant.

You'd have thought I had a begging bowl.
The rain lashes the windows.
Soon I'll eat, maybe forget the last train.

I came through the woods
as the hill road turned
the sea rinsed with pine

the horizon a ribbon of aquamarine.
Now I'm settled, expectant
and don't deserve this food.

All I did was stand in the rain
inquire politely.
You are tired, a lovely woman said

I'll check with my husband.
The room is fourteen new mats.
The tea is in a red pot

with a decent red spout.
A winsome daughter brought it in
says she's been to Ayer's Rock.

She's not heard of Uluru.
The sea is roaring plenty.
I can't get enough of this wasabi.

The chrysanthemums I finished at once.
But for a residue of mauve dressing
the crystal bowl's now empty

Ryōkan's still out there
in all weathers, admirable
Great Fool that he is.

Dumb Further North

A solitary
mountain sucks an icy wind
in from the sea.
Its crater has its feast of snow.

Pheasants break out of stubble —
mad running on paddy banks
their heat in their heads

tails up, stupid
veering in and out of alignment —
you'd think they remember
an earthquake.

A Cold Night in Kisakata

A warm bar, drinking sake and watching the sumo. The National Championships way down at Kyushu. One more drink and I'll walk down to the phone box near the station and ring the beloved. Feet like ice as the wind whips across the concrete floor of the half-open phone box. Chokai-san will be up there behind me, in the bitter dark, with its sleet. Under the volcano, I'll dream of a lost notebook. Then, with the storm, I surface with Bashō's ardour in mind, his 'weather-beaten skeleton' warming.

These flimsy walls
the lightening passes through them.
Body thunders with illumination.

I woke as a skeleton.
If you'd seen me then
each bone lit

certain I had the wit
to say the right poem
make words match lava

the sea's night sky
the stars shining
all the way to China.

As it was, I huddled back
into bedclothes
imagined myself

gloriously exposed
and unsafe —
a genuine traveller.

Party Train

It wasn't Kenji's Milky Way train. In the mountain air, it pulled in from the north, but did not bring the cold with it. Three carriages, blue, green and pink, each with a name painted on the side. FU, GETSU, HANA. Music. Moon. Flower. People eating drinking and singing in each. In the window of Music three woman look out, waving and smiling. You bow and smile, your hands together, and their hands meet under their tipsy faces. It's not even morning tea-time on the party train. Have they been laughing all night? As for the Moon carriage, it was pulling out before you could reach for the camera. In Flower there was a man at a mic…

So you missed the happiness shots.
The departure left you with old
images of peaks
bare fields and geese
but little by way of human stocks.

You hardly deserve to carry on.
What do you think life's about?
Get a grip on yourself.
The women are still waving —
your head's in the worn
dictionary.

Slowly the Special Express
— stopping at most stations! —
approaches the tunnel
under the choppy sea
to surface in Hokkaido
and more snow. O

Party Train from the deep north
with your happy, weather-beaten skeletons
battling for the microphone
flushed and plump
with enlightenment.

Leaving Sapporo

White fields, bright —
great hand-spans.

The idea of purity:
farm machinery under snow.

The fields slide away
from the noisy train.

Bodhidharma's teachings:
take in the snow falls.

Still the power lines
spark the train on.

Going north to find
your own invisible might.

The fields thickening
as you write.

Strange Joy

Transported
it's impossible to even doze
without feeling cleansed.

Drifts pile up.
You don't need to know
what you're leaving behind.

Lucid water in plastic
the bottle trembling in its holder.
Crystal lights — progress.

Imagine.
Tonight reaching
mid-stream Milky Way

Kenji there waiting.

Good News Near Shibetsu

Marvellous.
This could be your undoing —

hurl yourself into powder snow
it's as light as can be

stay where you fall in the drift
let the sun come back

melt what is there around you
be still there at night

for the crinkling and little cracks
sounding around your cheeks.

Then another snowfall
which you accept full-faced

like the last of the chrysanthemums
that you ecstatically ate.

You're on the slow train
for the loss of forms

Can't Remember Where I'm Staying Tonight

As the sun goes, the snow is getting its tombstone look.
Can't remember where I'm staying tonight.

No longer that blaze of light on the hills that are beyond the hills.
A long white pulsing rim was out there, holding to its edge.

The far-flung tip could be a jumping off point.
I'd be in that prison camp with Chekhov.

Wakkanai, the northern tip, another two hours off.

The river beside the track is a sheet of ice.
Shadowy green, the side of a fish.

Scales on its bank, the pale belly below.
It flicks its way north, making a sea of sky.

Wakkanai

All of a sudden people were getting off in the dark. Luckily I recognized the word for South. South was where I did not want to be.

Now you've arrived.
See what it actually is
in the perishing early evening.

Slush on a narrow street
as slippery as all shit.
Pong of crabmeat and kerosene.

A ferry's just left
for Vladivostok
its horn not short on lament.

After the sloppy udon
in the café near the station
the only toilet was —
back at the station!

You came
and then you went
nearly arse over tit
in the carpark.

And the name seems to mean
Young Home or New Home.
Not wacker as in 'you bloody wacker'

but the 'Wakka' you see
in 'Kindergarten.'
This written standing in the sleet

standing under the arches
of a colonnade, classical —
as if the place received

Romans
or ancient Greeks.
The Russians then.

It runs down to the sea
and there's only half of it
for the fishermen seeking a living

some order
on angry seas.
The bilingual brochure says

it's a pity you didn't get here earlier.
You missed Stella's Sea Eagles
and the soaring Berwick Swans.

And if you'd caught the Swan Festival
you'd have had raffle, bingo
and the speed-eating contest.

On Catching the Ferry to the Snow-capped Volcano on the Island of Rishiri

Wake in the dark
ready to embark
on the iron deck.

Ring your wife tonight
tell her you miss her.
Say you love the cold.

Sit out on the prow
let the wind blow
words back into the gullet.

Hope the sky will clear
the sleet cease
for your cone to appear.

Consume its fire
the ice of its rim
the snow on your lips.

A Morning Walk in a Spasm of Sunshine

Still with the taste of crabmeat
stepping over sea urchins —
a crow's footpath feast.

The rusty fleet sets off
late sun on the hulls
cormorants hanging back.

A tapestry of nets on cobbles
green green the deep
and the cobalt.

Fishing huts wrapped
like the idle craypots.
Nets for everything.

A settlement awaits summer
like that bent woman
who smiled as you passed.

Flotsam at the breakwater
debris at the canal mouth
a bank-up of shitty stuff.

A place at the limits
of tolerance.
Hush hush satellite links.

Russkies share the crab-meat.
Yanks monitor
watch towers.

The last of blinding light
makes a creamy wedge
of the departing ferry.

The 'Land Heart Ferry'
going out in
United Kingdom colours.

Lucid

These folk must carry sea-spray
into their bedclothes

have salt in their ears, their fingernails.
Every child is born a fish.

The day they marry they come good —
become something resembling you or me.

Then, in the dark of the wash
they spawn the length of the coast.

Born and re-born in this
'excessively lucid landscape'

After Sapporo, Travelling South Heading into Kenji Country

'Black hair soaked, packing rope soaked
You finally make it into the train compartment',
as he wrote in *Early Spring Monologue*.

Kenji's name is to die for:
Wise rule/temple.

'I have been under no illusions thus far
I have failed to live up to myself.'

'I have resolved time and again
To be alone
Unseen by anyone…'

At each page I shed the pong of crab-meat.

At one point, as the train slowed
a line shattered the glass of the window.
'The stars flutter again like a species of bird at the point of extinction'.

That Photograph

Nothing at all is dependable
Nothing at all can be counted on…
    Miyazawa Kenji, 'Burning Desires Past'

Kenji stands in the field
thinking of his lungs.
His boots are filling with blood.

A black blood
darker than the soil.
The humus of himself ready to spill

all over mother earth
and his sister's earth
the land he's shared since her passing.

The ground beneath could be sea.
The stars above him constitute his brilliance.
The Milky River will carry him home.

Meanwhile, what he can tell you about rocks
is what you love to know about plants.
His strength is mineral, his heart platinum.

When I read him I feel sub-atomic.
He puts me on the space ship Earth.
The poem seeks to be composed

in Siberian heavens, ice futures
and the snow on blades of grass
falls in flames… falls in flames.

Cherry Trees by the Kitakami River

Contorted, over cultivated?
Burnt by something other than themselves?

They are simply, strangely within themselves —
like dead poets, or poets waiting to blossom.

Some, half way up their trunk
have faces like bullfrogs.

Others pretend to be slow ruins.
Moss in the crutch is everlasting.

Like that one, I'd like my belly wrapped.
I want to be ready for any black wave.

And this limb has been freshly cut.
They have lacquered its gash.

The wound is a cluster
of oblongs and recesses —
honeyed escarpment, like the cliffs at Bamiyah.

Through the dying reeds
almost straw, the river flows
snakes over the apron of Iwate-san.

Insomnia in Sendai

In striking distance from Tokyo —
an easy ride for the well slept
sloth for those who want more sleep.

O they are good at it
all along the carriage they could be
dying quietly, as if it's
already taken place, the aftermath evacuation.

Now you'd say they were preparing
for the grubby indigo
wave, the one that rolled
up the river at Shiogama
the salt port, insouciant

as if it had side-swiped, already engulfed
all things beautiful
at Matsushima, crushing
the wisdom of pines

taking the oldest temples
with it before
picking up the boats and cars
sweeping them

universally west
towards the waiting hills
the valleys and mountains or any ledge
to deposit sheds schools houses

the litter
of living and dead things
scattered on the coast
you in your sleeplessness were
thinking to travel, seeking

right wakefulness
and all the rest of it before the burials
and cessation of movement when

there are no eyes, no ears, no tongue, no body, no mind
no colour, sound, or smell
no taste, no touch, no thing

no realm of sight, no realm of thoughts
no ignorance, no end of ignorance
no old age, no death

no end to old age and death
no suffering, nor any cause of suffering, nor end to suffering
no path, no wisdom, no fulfilment

Leaving Ise

Dusk and moist ground.
The boxy houses shuttered.

A snow-sky over there, beyond Nara
or in Kyoto where my poor books wait.

The river we just crossed was a dark mirror
its reflections hidden: everyone's treasure.

I'm still harbouring the aromas of sawn timber
sweet off-cuts

by the immaculate carpenters
repairing pavilions, adding

gifts of the earth
to the scent of the forest.

It's true that I found
The Inner Stall to the Sacred Horse:

no lusty piebald, but pungent dung aplenty.
And there was the *Outer Stall to the Sacred Horse*:

spotless. Both stalls near *The Hall of Pure Fire*.
But I did not see *The Hall of Pure Fire*.

Somehow, for the life of me it escaped me.
And I lack the milk to pour into the fire.

3

Cicadas

All Over the Body, Hands and Eyes

You get to the old place at midnight
a three quarter moon burning high to the south
its heat wrapped in a smoky gauze.
The gate unlatched for you to bow
into your grass hut.

The bedroom gushes and hums.
The Otowa river roars in its race
a garden seethes with cicadas.
In the corner, a bed
under the window, paper screens

opening onto the sunken garden:
as if you might rest your head
in a forest clearing. Further up
in a millennial temple
a flame to peace still burns.

You scatter gear all over room.
It's not your gompa just yet.
Before nodding off in the heat
reading Dōgen's *The Issue at Hand* —
'flowers fall when we cling to them

and weeds only grow when we dislike them'.
The cicadas rattle their way
into the root of your skull.
You wake facing the bamboo
in the eastern window, waterfall-green.

Summer, and not a flower to be seen.
'When there is a single cataract in the eye
flowers in the sky show each way…
it is eyes throughout the body.'
Dōgen's words shimmer in the bamboo.

At dusk, when the cicadas resumed —
metallic resoundings in forest.
This morning — mid-morning and steamy already —
a continuous high-pitched hum
a high and low in unison, a stream of unbreakable

sound, a vibration arising from earth
hangs in the air as agitation, assault
a rattling of weaponry.
No birdcall makes an impression on it.
You just have to start the day, face the music.

Unholy

One morning
      all these beginnings
           early enough to be fresh
                it was an awakening of sorts

you confessed to unholy
      satisfaction
           in the body by the fly-wire door:
            that it was dead.

Hanging there
      as if on a sticky thread
           on the grey matter
                of an old paling.

You marvelled at it, this flimsy
      proof of extinction
           so transparent
                in the light.
                A husk of violence.

All that was left, say
      of a spirited life.

A notation of the body —
      it had emptied itself out
           to become a remnant
                as empty of song
                if it was a song
           as life itself

if life has a self.

Pillow

<u>Concentration</u> *is actualisation, it is expression, it is night time when* <u>one reaches back for the pillow.</u>
        Dōgen, *Ocean Seal Concentration*.

1
You reach back, but for what —
in order to return to Hiroshima?

You were young, it was your birthday, 25
you were travelling with your
first wife, blonde and already boring
to your callow self.

You gave yourself a chocolate bar
ate it at the railway station
having seen everything
hand in hand
in the museum, at the Peace Park

then promenading in the sunlight
under a platinum sky
it was a hot summer then, too
it's always a blazing summer
in Hiroshima

the young loves you were
stood before the eternal flame
the know-all inscription
that implicates everybody
and nobody:
LET THE SOUL REST IN PEACE
FOR WE SHALL NOT REPEAT THIS EVIL

Whereas here
at this late stage of the journey
you only have to imagine yourself

if you can bear to imagine yourself
lying on the forest floor —

'all over my body are hands and eyes
throughout my body are hands and eyes...'

Crawling with knowledge.

2
Remember that abysmal title
          Hiroshima Mon Amour?
In the beginning, like an awakening, a continuous
shot of a man and woman making love.

Their lingering touches, filling the mind to the brim
                with exploratory meaning.
The skin of each naked body mottling, or something.

        Sand, you thought.

They'd come out of the sea, rolled in the dunes
or the wind from the dunes had blown up
and was sprinkling sand on them
grain by grain as they made love.

           Their skin clears again
and a new suite of touches
promises to carry the love-making to a climax...

It never dawned on you that
on the shoulders and arms
and backs of the lovers
                it was falling ash.

You saw nothing in Hiroshima, he says
when she opens her mouth to speak.

     I saw *everything*.
Everything, she whispers, as if speaking into a pillow.

     To think:
You were a couple who loved the touch, the whole feel of Japan.
Its food, raw and cooked, its purities, and purifications
its slow brewing of tea for small cups, the lowering of the body
into scalding water and the resting of it on grass mats.
The wonder at what the body could stand by way of heat
the tub's silky timber, smooth as skin scrubbed
pink through and through, ready for sleep as for lovemaking
the genitals as declared, ancient and tender
the way they are in prints by Utamaro.

3
Anybody would think the love
       between a man and a woman
       trumps all else.

3
Another DVD for keeping the cicadas at bay:
In *Rashōmon* Kurosawa instructs
his cameraman to shoot into the sun.

You see the woodcutter running though patches of light
   heart-beat flickering, his face
   intermittent below the canopy
or lit by the strategic placement
of mirrors in the wood:
the mirrors brought the sun in from a distance.

4
Turning the mind around and shining back (Dōgen).

Bashō's Sin

was leaving that child
by the side
of the road.

Only a larger Taoism
will do
to explain it.

'Hiroshima' —
pages in my mind
are peeling away.

I'll go there…
try to be naked, but
this promiscuity of speech —

summer downpours.
The 'plum rain'
is barren.

I'll discover, I hope
the character
for my own shame.

The word for Peace
is made of Roof
over Woman.

Another character
has the signs for Rice
and Mouth.

In the grass hut
I strive to be nobody
a hungry artist, unavoidably

walking in
my father's steps —
left left right

left left right
until I am bored
witless and lost.

'We must be steadfast
to survive history'.
Yes yes yes.

Anyway, I'm afraid
of not feeling a thing.
And of the word-rush nonetheless —
an after-blast.

If I am going
in good faith
it will knock me down
burn me through.

The sound-wave hit them first —
nothing but the cosmos.
Words hung in the air
smelling like sardines.

All the above, I say
as I gather myself
for the return
are my literary effects.

Rough Notes

1
A ghost just got on the bus.

His skin is paper
like a dead cicada.

Barely a body
apart from its trappings
their semblance of weight:

the umbrella, the black smock over his robe
the silk socks in which his toes
divide for the temple slip-ons.
And the feline handbag, from which he pulls
his sheet of tickets
tearing off two hundred yen's worth.

2
The train races south in the glare of sun.

You're swaying along recalling
Wilfred Burchett the Communist
who once so loved
the silver hulls of B29s.
His packed carriage rattled
with the samurai swords and daggers
of Japanese officers.

Do not smile for fear of seeming
to gloat at their surrender!
The sharing of fags lifted the mood.
A swig of sake
put everyone to rights.

And how canny he was
to detect the lies
of the Yank's top brass.

3
1.30 pm.
A café at the Hiroshima station.
How did you get here so quickly?
As if you'd fallen backwards —
still twenty-five and sugar-starved.

Burchett arrives at an empty shell
an exit of rickety gates.
Detained, he shows them
his typewriter, the letter

of introduction to the epicentre
sight unseen —
heading there on foot
along the river
where so many called
'water, water,' from the water.

4
THE ATOMIC PLAGUE
I write this as a warning to the World
DOCTORS FALL AS THEY WORK
Poison gas fear: All wear masks

5
The station's a lovely concourse
shining in the sun.
The sea is behind you
the gentle hills in the middle distance.

The seven rivers run clear.
The trams criss-cross the sparkling
waters once so clogged.

Almost Forgetting

Ogura writes — with a touch of shame —
of the bomb's 'monstrous magnificence'
the 'pageant of clouds' after the blast.

Surveying the city on the second day
'the sensation' was of 'looking down into a volcanic crater'
which was 'further advanced by the dark of night falling.'

The bright juxtaposition of the Milky Way
and the other stars in the night sky
with the fiery ruins below
gave such an impression
of 'primordial grandeur'

'it almost made me forget my worries about you' —
speaking of his wife and children.

Of mothers, he observes
dementia at the loss of their children.
For days in their arms they carry dead children.

Untitled

Think of your mother's puffy ankles
her skin peeling around them
like her old stockings.

Think of her being
a nanosecond from your dear self —
a black patch, in sticky tar…

When the peace crowd thins
you can go in search
of the *atomic shadow.*

Poor Reason

In Kawabata's exquisite, private collection —
a hand, by Rodin.

Here is 'the thinker'
incinerated on the steps of a bank.

His shadow is the thing.
A bleaching of thought —

the press of poor reason
into the quartz.

Boy O Boy

Batter by hand, O three person'd God
                    John Donne

Oppie the live-wire.

Oppie the *Destroyer of Worlds*.

Oppie the Red, Oppie the Astro Boy
who predicted black holes, Mad Oppie
who left a poisoned apple for his rival.

Oppie who strutted his *High Noon*.
Oppie besotted at Point Zero
in love with *Trinity*.

Oppie and his numbers men.
'Aint God Great' —
at the math that came out right.

And the top-secret news
reached Potsdam:
'The baby was born.'

Secretary of State Stimson
so happy he might have given
birth to it himself.

And Dwight slumped and said
the secret code said
'The lamb is born

or some damn thing like that'.
Back in the desert Oppie cried:
'Oh my, this is hard on the heart.'

'Now we are the sons of bitches'
was the murmur from his
ever so bright men.

Like Grass

On the plaque of the monument
near the bridge with its contortions
simulating the suffering of steel
the writing is carved
into the marble —
'grass style'
beautifully light in gestural presence.

It tells of hair.
Hair lost at a snail's pace
compared to hair piled into a cabinet.
Hair lost over two weeks, say…

To some
the resemblance to a monk's tonsure
was striking. Then, as soon as fifty
days after the blast
it could grow again.

Crazy Iris

How the Humanist
— like Ibuse's 'crazy iris' —
springs up in one.

From the *Oriental Hotel*
you step out into Heiwa Avenue.
Take a left into the shady lane
find it does not have the stench
of death, only the sky-high
pictures of girls
who will dance with you.

It's broiling heat, the same clutch
of words thrum in the skull.
You've heard that
today
for the first time in sixty years
the US Ambassador will arrive
at the Peace Park.

Even so
hundreds already stream
towards the fully grown, green trees
occupied with battalions
of cicadas.

Canopy upon canopy around the concourse.
You did not know the war had spared so many.
Every seat occupied, the ground littered
with veteran men and women
each with a time piece.

And then the long, green, humid wait.

Silence is suddenly upon us.
All of us.
Everyone standing with their hats off
heads bowed
to the toll of the bell.

A wild thought at 8.15:
consider each cicada as a sentient being.

In the same instant birds ignited mid-air.
Mosquitos and flies, squirrels
family pets crackled
and were gone.

'What stillness!
voices of the cicada
penetrate the earth.' (Bashō)

City of Angels

It (Hiroshima Diary) is written like a work of Japanese literature: precision, tenderness, and responsibility are its essential qualities... a form of writing indispensable today... — Elias Canetti, *Conscience of Words*

Dr Michihiko Hachiya, the Director
of the Hiroshima Communications Hospital
revises his meaning for 'devastation'...

people think it's the end of the world
they are standing among the dead
this is the collapse of the earth
everything seems dark, dark all over...

The framed photograph of the Emperor
is carried through the rubble
of bodies, across razed ground
and stowed in the bowels
of the castle.

After *that*
would have been the moment
to release their own supreme, scientific bombs
on California, on the enemy's
City of Angels.
Alas.

The life re-affirming spasm passed.
The dying were delivered
to the fly-ridden wards
the pus of vengefulness
washed out by the first cyclone.

His hospital overflowed with the dishevelled.
'I felt ashamed to be well dressed.'

Each body, thereafter, received as a *person*.

Eyes All the Way Down

Compose yourself before the life-sized ones:

a clutch of survivors in rags
huddling at a bus stop, the camera allows you
to wait like Yoshito Matsushige —
strangely calm, wanting
to get closer.

'I took about ten steps forward
and wanted to snap another
but the scenes were so gruesome
my viewfinder clouded with tears.'

You can step back now, go outside
back to the enormous space
enjoyed by the concourse, why
even the *Hibakusha*
the remaining bomb-damaged ones
were sat in the front row.
Hard to believe they were out there
under the summer sky, in the blazing sun.

And look, look, here comes
the good Doctor Hachiya.
He is dreaming again
among the bodies, heaped in piles
all of them staring at him.
'I saw an eye sitting
on the palm of a girl's hand.'

You should, now
keep this to yourself
or people will think you mad
or confusing being in the peace park

with that hair-raising
scientific summation
of the desert blast with its 'eyeball'
in the middle of the shockwaves
as the fission gathered momentum
in its millionths of a second.

 'Before the radiation leaked away
conditions within the eyeball
resembled the state of the universe
moments after its first
primordial explosion.'
In the next instant
Dr Hachiya
saw the eyeball leap
from the palm of his hand
into the sky, come back towards him
so that looking up, he could see
'a great bare eyeball
bigger than life
hovering over my head
staring point blank at me.'

Later, when you went underground
down the ramp near
the timeless inscription
to stand before the moving
wall of the dead, the mug shots
appearing and disappearing
only to roll around
on view again in the dark —

you were like the good doctor:
'...powerless to move.'

The White Horse

Om, the dawn, verily, is the head of a sacrificial horse,
the sun the eye, the wind the breath, the open mouth —
    Brihadaranyaka Upanishad

One evening
in a lane on my way
back to the Oriental Hotel
I saw a white horse.
Glowing like snow in the dusk.

A man beside a frilly carriage
groomed its silky mane
the quivering neck
and muscular haunch
with his brush and comb.

A huge horse-eye
glistened under the street lamp.
A sea-breeze
helped me back to my room

where I slept open-mouthed
awoke to the universe
of a museum
with a girl at a desk.

Excuse me
O excuse me, I am sorry.
Sir, how can I help? I said:
For ages I've had a picture in my head.

So horrible I don't want to say.
But now that I am here…
Dozu, dozu, she said.
Please, please.

It is of a horse that was once alight.
A horse without its…
She was, in the Japanese way
in the flow of my sentence.

Skin, she said.
Yes, a horse with its hide burnt off.
Does that image exist
or have I just imagined it?

Yes, it is true.
It was here, half of it.
(Did she mean half of the horse
or half of the picture?)

Damaged.
So many photographs
were taken of it. It was removed
I don't know where it is now.

It was in a cabinet?
Yes.
The exhibit itself
the material thing, was damaged by the flash?

Yes, she said.
Hiroshima had many horses.
And not only horses were damaged
we had many birds and dogs.

To Speak of Tragedy

That the speeches in the Peace Park
settled into the late morning
hum and husk-making
of cicadas, those survivors
making ashes of the mind.

Lines Found in My Father's Hiroshima Folder

Among his foolscap papers —
tucked into a report to the central committee
of the Metal Workers Union
there's a spectacular poem
printed in East Berlin
as bitter as Brecht
murderous of hope.

I rather think he'd be embarrassed now.
I bet that when he flew
from Tokyo to Hanoi
in 1972
from Peace-Conference to the B52s
he'd have forgotten about the poem

but once back home
he'd have pulled it out
to contemplate what no-one in the movement
could afford to say. He tried
as I try now to imagine the words
spoken by a woman, in her Japanese.

Ah yes, this year
I lack energy.
Peace! Peace!
I am tired of hearing about it.
I am exhausted with unreliability.
Disappearing into a deep sky, and
done in with fretfulness
unable to find the answer,
no matter how loud
I yell and cry.

I have become sick of everything.
The more uproarious the people,
the emptier my heart is…

Fukuda Sumako
called her poem
'Talking to Myself'.

Hibakusha

By the twisted rail
she alighted, bird-like
parked her veteran pushbike
its tyres pumped up hard.

She flicked through
the pages of a little notebook:
rows and columns
insect kanji squeezed in —
the almost squashed certifications.

It was like the rent book
my mother carried
in her hot purse during summer.

A tiny lady proud, somehow
expectant of me
as we rested in the clammy shade.
She'd shown me her regular
payments for damages.

Together we sat awhile
trying to cool in the late breeze.
We were the patient, the quiet ones
like weary peace-activists

as late model survivors streamed
out of town across the sparkling river
rushing headlong into the setting sun.

Brollies and visors for the lucky ones.
Forever parched those with a mind
for recalling 'water water.'
The skin of my friend lizard tough.

Damned I was
when she bundled up her things —
just cleared off
at my request for a photograph.

The Loveliest Things

were sighted earlier that morning
and later the same day.

Three spotless men escorting a trolly:

each conducting himself
preciously before and aft
keeping the sail cloth —

no, it could have been silk
draped over an object
as fat as an ox

which suddenly revealed
a part of its body as bronze
its lower lip as a bell.

Furthermore, at the last tolling

as the crowd dispersed
and the flowers, near the flame
rested in each other's arms

you looked across the concourse
saw the sliver of orange
heard the first beat

and the chant that belonged

to the monk who led the others
who held his fan, his drum
as an offering of notes

the drumming being the offering
the chanting being the peace-making
the line of saffron robes

a body as strong as an ox.

4

Dōgen's Ashes

Solitary Heron

Born of snow
purity O purity.

And still you're trying
to get to the root
of mind —

looking for a clean cut
in. And now this streak
standing mid-river

among the thriving sedge.
Stupidly you reached
for the camera

did not even pause
to let the bird —
…for itself…

A cyclist arrived
punishing the cobblestones.
You shift, only to look up

and the bird's gone.
Last thing was it's circling
over there…

as if gaining
the other shore
leaving you for dead.

Kite

In its turning circle you don't see its 'black ears'
any more than you see the whiskers of a rat in water.

In profile, on the bare branch of a tree, up towards the hill temples
you spot the beak, the useful hook of a garbage collector.

When it's overhead you don't think 'black'
not even at dusk. You see the lovely pale donkey brown.

And its flight is as soft — downy.
Its silence spreads itself over the gurgling river.

Except for that moment near the bridge at Sanjo-Dori.
Mid sky mid river mid your contemplative walk

its wings flap-snapped open like a spinnaker
like an attack on your face, the sound was behind it diving.

Nothing followed. It was swallowed by night.
You would never know the tale of it golden —

its flying arrival at dawn for the first Emperor:
its blinding of enemies, its war service.

Egret

It's not even standing at a sensible angle to the river:
beak neither facing downstream
nor into the flow of fish. It's askew, the hulk wedged

the head re-coiled so that
it's slack on the dowdy shelf of itself.
A study in oddball patience, non-expectation.

We'd been talking about the pace of Noh plays
and of the way the ghost or the ghost of a ghost
bears witness: the vantage point being the thing.

But its stillness, so unobserved, seems post-ghost.
Its dream if it has one is way up river
its own witness, standing indifferent to drama.

Impossible bird! But then
as if suddenly fed up with our spectatorship
it drops, stone-grey, a curtain.

An inner wing cleaves to that outer wing
and a long night cloak has fallen —
a twin-panelled shroud.

Majestically erect in attendance upon itself
sword drawn, its feet are powerfully still
in the river's rushing inks.

Savagely it knit-picks its breast, stretches
stabs at the autumn sky
wounding the emptiness over cold waters.

Ritual Sharing

Your coat is beautiful, but where's your brain?
                Attar, *The Conference of the Birds.*

Three terraces in the gurgling river:
a conference of birds.

Upstream, a protest of gulls.
Downstream, the royal herons.

A commune of ducks in between.
The gulls are not going to budge.

You'd have to tear-gas them.
The ducks duck and water smother

slippery as rats, a glint
of teal under wing redeems them.

One heron, the male, has a black cap
split by its white stripe.

It is single-pointedly looking upstream —
its life depending on it.

If the river freezes
it will still be there, just so.

Its mate, that perfect snow study
snakes about in the wash, wading and peering.

When she pulls her head back
you could make a ceremony

with the bow of her neck.
For a time, like a student of history

she props, looking upstream
downstream, insouciant with regard to her fisherman.

Ceremonially timid, she turns
raises languid wing beats

lands near him in silent
heart ritual.

If I walk on, just leave them be
what will become of me?

Rakushisha

I couldn't find the house until I was helped by a stranger, and even then, I ended up approaching it from behind. It was near a graveyard, and a plot of aged persimmon trees. 'His roofs are buried under the branches of overgrown persimmon trees', Bashō wrote, of Kyorai's house. The sun made each of the fruit glow. In front of the house there was the empty field in alignment with Mt Hiei, on the other side of town, where I slept. I peered into the house, and saw myself preparing a meal, shuffling and bending at the small iron stove.

To find the disciple's house
walk though the limelight
of the bamboo grove.
Inhale the mould.

Don't stop
or birds in the high
wash of green
will carry you off in shrillness.

At Tenryū-ji
keep to the path by the pond
pass along the verandah
leave the priests where they belong.

Show your indifference
to koans
until a persimmon thumps
the back of your neck.

Paint your face yellow.
Arrive in a storm.
Rest your travel-weary self
at the diminutive gate.

Then step right in.
You're here.

Pretend no one's at home.
Come in out of the rain
say nothing, listen!

What you can hear
are the welcoming verses
tumbling out of their rack
like fresh vegetables.

A mat your size —
hardly bigger than your satchel
is laid out to dry
on the hearth by the grate.

Put the kettle on.
Make the tea.
Taste the tea.

If you've arrived
soliciting memorable lines
toss those out with the leaves.

Curling into Each Other's Smoke

At dusk, walking home up the aqueduct
the foothills of Hiei-san
hold to their distinctions.

The russet of maple marks itself
off from the ginger beech
the gulleys hold to their ash.

And the plump wagtail
(almost as big as our mudlark)
is a black-backed wedge

with a white trimmed wing
which, when it takes off —
a fan doing its quick work.

Just then, as the bird vanished
two boys flapped past
on their bikes —

black rain jackets flying
their clean *ghi* showing
wild and white underneath:

off to karate as the girls arrived —
two twelve-year-olds
curling into each other's smoke

their spirits so lit
laughter came out of them
like fire crackers.

Down the race their
trail of smiles.
No bird could surpass them.

Some U.S. General
should get an agreement
to parachute them into a war zone

where all on the ground
no matter their grievance
would seek to make peace.

You walk on, into the dusk.
You reach the spot behind
the teahouse in this garden

and it was a clean dark.
The hill-mist came to meet you
got into your neck.

Then along comes
the jogger in aqua —
aqua and a white cap

his waterproof pants apple green
giving the body within
its disgusting sauna.

Sodden Thrush

Sopping leaf-litter.
You might have thought her bogged —
then prised herself

gained flight with an insect whirr
a kind of skid into the air
yet egg-heavy underneath.

Hugging the bank
she covered ground from one
end of the garden to the other.

No song.
A flurry of silence.
Her middle loose as a bonbon

she landed with a quick rustle.
A watchful refusal
of song.

Listening Out

Burton Watson heard the uguisu
in the woods around here.
Its call, *tani-watari*,

carried it across
one valley into another.
Yesterday, in Tokyo

we meet again at the mosaic
of *Guernica*, in the plaza
of the Maruzen building

and we saunter, like old golfers
over the road to eat noodles
in a café by Central Station.

Business men blow cigarette smoke into broth.
Head-banded young workers off construction sites
swagger in bell-bottoms, blowing steam.

Is Burton looking out for Billy Budd?
Pleased he is that I've spotted
his new baseball cap.

He drawls, speaks softly, he says *commen-
tary* slowly, giving the whole train
of tertiary considerations time

to occupy the platform. He waves it off.
His translations have little truck with that.
He'll just rivet what the text does

buff its steel and wholegrain —
primed for a flower
Pound might've pinned to his soft lapel.

Last time, he insisted on walking me
to General's MacArthur's Imperial Hotel.
He remembers the nearby gardens scorched.

He remembers failing to translate the mantra
of the Heart Sutra. *Gate, Gate, Prajnaparamita Gate.*
Who in their right mind tries to nail that *beyond?*

You just can't do it. No one can.
As if to say: translation is sitting at the piano.
You can only dream of fingering the beyond.

Debris

Bashō's *Iro no Hama*, is the 'coloured beach,' as one writer calls it, with 'some pink shells'. Bashō wants us to *listen* to the waves hiss and scrape as a litter of 'petals, tiny shells.' He went to see the harvest moon, when the 'bush clover,' as others insist on calling it, blew through the warm air into the shallows. Yesterday, when I was there, the water was cold, pure crystal (no sign of the old nuclear power station just around the point). Bashō came home slowly, like driftwood, unworried as to what was debris and what not.

You set off from his little temple close to the raggedy shore.
Strolling between the sea and the huts — gal-iron, rust

timber worn as a fisherman's face, there are pontoons
out on the flat water, cages beneath them, fish fattening.

Nets and craypots one side of the path, a woman's washing line
on the other. Everything closed, nothing for sale

the belly goes empty between one point and the next.
Sun high over the shell-grit — full dazzle.

To appease the summer you walk into the sea:
the inlet's an island, you're as good as naked, better than naked

the waves hiss, the petals the tiny shells are yours.
The hungry path joins a road up to the saddle.

In the hills the on-coming cement trucks are apple green.
Hair-pin bends, drivers bowing at their wheels:

startled by the vagabond making progress, wet underpants
in the sling of a t-shirt, heat bearing down on the hero.

Gassho. Gassho, you are paying respects to the mountain and to the sea!
And it's always a path between huts and shells, the petals —

what's in the poem is in the mind, all that's there is plain as day.
Pot plants at steps, clay deities with plump bellies —

you're making a pig of yourself on potato chips
your mouth is salty, it will do you no good, water water.

In a cage by an open door, two parrots sleep.
Yellow as butter, short-tailed, a coral rim around the eyes.

Speechless when they wake. Live birds, dead poets.
And a woman squats by the path, strong in the neck and buttock.

The wide blade of her knife stripping a fish from its spine.
'Konichewa.'   'Konichewa.'

And fruity the trucky who dropped, on a turn, his soft porn.
You gave the mag. a scan. The women mere girls and the sun's too bright.

I pack no provisions for my long journey, entering emptiness
in the midnight moon — and still you don't know, any more than Bashō

what to put in and what to leave out, literary or not.
All the way little jetties stump into the water, brutally concrete.

Two men seem to be fishing for the hills across the bay.
A girl catches a minnow and squeals for her boy who squats on a box.

The sun's going down, singing the trees, sinks over China.
A swathe of shadow, like a war cloud, sets on the shingles.

The traveller can lift his sail-cloth! There's a warm patch
on the far side of the bay, the last searching light

into cages, illuminations of catch, each spec
of desire, all scales and shells, the clover on a promontory

in its dusk. Rock, pine out of rock, pipe-cleaners in profile
water shadows and hawk-eagles for company:

lone pines in a desert of sea, their whistling
above and beyond, calling needles in thin air.

A chill full moon lolls over the hotel.
Hot springs fill the baths downstairs.

Lyric Yellow

Back in Kyoto you walked home through the shrine. Through the torii there was a young man meditating under a tree: a gaikoku-jin, like yourself, honouring the tree for all it was worth. Around him you went — on leaves the colour of mustard seed, saffron, lemon, lime. Looking back, into the sun, he was sitting on a bed of gold. A pale gold, like the robes of the monks at Koya-san. There, too, the leaves had yellowed, the robes of the monks with them. No mysteries.

The man at the tree was as straight as a good lyric.
'Even in an age gone bad, the lyric way stays straight.'

At Koya-san, Saigyō's 'meditation hall'
was as small as a grass hut.

He couldn't have stored
a bow for his defence, let alone

practice his old court knife-thrust.
His shelter thus a peace hut, and locked.

As the weather broke
you stood with the schoolgirl

who led you to the spot. Gassho —
and each of you bowed to snow and to poetry.

She went her way
you climbed the elephant steps of the pagoda —

in under eaves, ripe as an orange grove.
The pines announced green to its glow.

Inside — Buddha's among thick columns; womb-realm.
The diamond-realm also, a hide and seek between the two.

O you don't get more than the crazy drift of the discourse.
You want to, but who doesn't wish for arcane marriage

in heaven? Your lips half numb, the gift
was looking out across the temple grounds —

snowfalls in flurries, the whole space teased
by spirals, puffs and ground drifts, and the quiet

music among the trees, their great spines
standing and standing simply.

No tricks, 'no language-mind challenges'
as Snyder said of Saigyō.

Rain in Kyoto

1
Bird calls and the Otawa river:
dimpled notes, continuous song.
In the sunken garden
you step across a green bridge —
moss-footed, lichen-tongued.

2
Morning waking
with the thumbs of coos
pressing on your temples.

One, then another —
easing into a rhythm that finds
the mantra of the pulse.

An oldish man might become
almost young again.
More rain for the river.

Last night it carried on rushing
down from the hills
filling the town with plenty.

On the embankment at Shingo-dori
ten thousand teenagers mingled without rancour —
loosened their ties for the weekend.

3
Slide the door open
let in the morning roar.

The sound of water widens.
Each fat drop rings true —
keeps on opening.

An avalanche offers
to orchestrate itself, then doesn't.
The waters fall as trees fall
at the end of their lives.

4 *Waking Happens in Reservoirs*

After walking back from Shisendo, The House of Chinese Immortals (more poets!), with the hills up ahead smoking, you sit in the middle room, looking into the garden, the river rumbling and rushing down on itself just over there, beside the Imperial Villa, the doves cooing further up the slope. They seem to be in the same place as yesterday and the day before. Maybe they have a nest there, except that it's not the season for nests. Maybe they have taken shelter from the rains, which have been coursing through your sleep for two whole nights. Peace.

These doves, they add to the smoke of Hiei-san.
That mist in their throats, their slow deep music.

Water off wide eaves heals the mind —
wakes you before dawn, dove-tuned.

Water off wide eaves returns to the earth happily —
fat splashes on pebbles in lovely runnels.

A surge plays on and off-key, mainly on.
A gurgling wins over words, almost pings

dances down, pocks stone, hums, plucks
little hollows from time like flames.

You soften and sleep, soften and fall back to sleep.
The waking happens in reservoirs of temples.

5 *Stand at the threshold, be inside outside*

Feathers and hissing rain
gleaming leaves and pebbles —
put names to the long sounds
break their sheaths of silence.

(The silence beneath, behind what you heard all night.)

Now, out on the courtyard —
a bright scree of water
comes down soft and hard
cools the mind
warms it at the same time.

(You were warm all night. The rain calmed the mind).

One drop slows, and you are in it.
Another composes its fall —
you are to be shattered and
reassembled, hollow as a coo.

Waterfall, womb-call.

(Good Watson-san, stopping at the mantra).

6 *The Character for 'River'*

Each day, my strapping adult son has been rising early to scramble up Hiei-san, coming down even faster to find himself among monkeys. For days, too, I have been anticipating his departure, and the clearing it will leave in me. I don't know what I will do with that emptiness. This morning we went to the little hut Buson built for Bashō up the back of Konpuku-ji, the temple where Bashō, when he was not much younger than my son, learnt calligraphy, the Chinese classics and Zen, that essential mix of what must be mastered and what must be let go. Then we parted: my son to do a farewell walk along the river, me to make my way back here. I sat

in a coffee shop, trying to make out a few things from a Japanese edition
of *Snow Country*, only recognizing the character for 'river'.

Go back now, leave the pathetic *patisserie*.
Take the narrow path
up towards Hiei-san, dusk rising.

Climb with your back to the old avenues
with their thousand years of steps —
the ancient grid for devotions.

Alone in the kitchen you can
get the miso going
check out the packet of tofu.

You can stand by the stove
adjust the soup to a simmer
have a quiet drink.

Then you can step outside to wait
on the path with the pines.

When he comes, even in the dark
you'll make out his shape
leaning into the steepening slope —

and maybe slowing, as you do
at the last of the vegetable patches
and the orchard glistening with berries.

A good trick, these recent nights of drizzle
is to step out from the trees and drift
down in his direction
the brolly held cleverly.

How long does it take
on a civilized evening
for a son to spot a father's commotion?

7 *Kelp*

After the rain, when the sun hits the trees, the light spreads like fire and crimson dances with black, beats like a drum. So many reds, in actuality — madder, vermilion, scarlet, crimson-violet, a red that laps in ultramarine, a red in wood-shadow — but always that red which makes its secret marriage with black. It's hard to find the line between art and fury, between order and time's rough passing.

So what's it to be? More slap-dash meditation
or a return to leaf-litter and the vice of poetry?
A quality of silence or a setting to with the rake
as if words can be truly ordered?

Yesterday you heard yourself read.
The room was brighter than day.
You should have asked for an X-ray
of each person's heart.

As it was, you put a few wagtails into the air.
Then, in the void that followed —
your curse that you were there not here
on the mat, which is all the more lonely!

Bashō and Saigyō struggled with this pathos.
Should words burn in their own time?
Or are they native to thoughts we have
without words (even in airless, fluorescent rooms)?

The local poets can't make you feel right.
Your reds are different. Your leaves stay dry
year by year waiting for their fire.
When you burn you incinerate culture.

Trust yourself more. Pour vodka, *Absolut*.
Know your own autumn. Get home to your wife.
And tomorrow, when you arrive at Saigyō's
hall of 'awesome nightfall'

play possum with what you know
with what's in the old bones —
the sea's roar and the reds of its weeds:
inscriptions on the kelp of your tongue.

A Son Arrives and Departs

I set up the Buddha
in the room he'd slept in —
mat facing west
teahouse and garden to the north.

The sun sets over the lovely
eaves of the house below.
Smoke of incense coils
coils towards the dusk.

Then it is dark. Some bird
with the thinnest of peeps
moves around the house
to the smoke. Both cease.

What was it?
Where did he go?
The man who was once a boy.
This father who hardly knows himself.

He loved the space of the room.
The mats and panels, the symmetry
of screens that spoke
to the safety he needs.

Each day, hour by hour
when he was not climbing the mountain
I was getting to know his cone of silence.
Then he had to leave.

Going and Coming

As the years pass
I travel further and further
from my children.
I miss them sorely.

I imagine that they prepare
for my death.
That is good.
They are growing up.

Yet still I pine.
One phone call
from across oceans
pulls me back home.

I travel on
preparing and preparing.
I remember when I said
goodbye to my parents.

They were stalwart —
half knowing I barely
intended to return.
My children are kinder.

Big Root Feast

On the west side of town
near the steps of a temple
there's more white flesh
this time steaming in caldrons
heavy women sweating beside them
their domesticated men assisting
everyone happy keeping winter at bay
the big root offerings with Kanji
carved into the season's sacrifice
the celebrants warmed, ageing
on the spot, devouring, slurping
until silence befalls their bowls.

Nothing Gained

Ko Un told you that
at Daitokuji in Kanazawa
behind the altar
there's an urn
with Dōgen's ashes in it.

True? True, he said.
His good straight smile.
Snyder was there:
they'd done a reading
before the altar.

Ko Un had, afterwards
casually found himself
behind the offerings
holding the urn
with Dōgen's ashes in it.

Soon you were tunnelling
through coastal range
and autumn rain
to the Sea of Japan —
lovely weathered Kanazawa.

You found your way between
grave stones, napkinned Jizus
and stood
like a tale-teller in *Rashōmon*
vital in a storm, barely out of the storm

battering the temple steps.
The huge doors were locked.
No one came to your calls.
You were there for moons.
All you managed to see

peering through a pane
with a grill at the rear
of the temple
was into the gloom
of some corridor, or hall.

But such inexplicable happiness
as you rattled home to Shugakuin!
Everyone in the carriage
with their eyes closed.

Who's to know what honours what?

Notes

Lucid
'excessively lucid landscape', Miyazawa Kenji (1896-1933), 'Scenery and Music Box'; this translation and those below by Roger Pulvers' *Strong in the Rain, Selected Poems* by Kenji Miyazawa (2007)

After Sapporo, Travelling South, Heading into Kenji Country
'I have been under no illusions thus far...' *Departure to a Different Road*
'I have resolved...' *Night*
'Like a species of bird...' *Jealous of the Dawn*

That Photograph – was taken in c.1928 by Hiroshi Oshima, and the last lines of the poem are from *Hill Daze*.

Insomnia in Sendai
...'there are no eyes...' etc is from the *Heart Sutra*, often recited at fune-ral services.

Almost Forgetting
Toyofumi Ogura's *Letters from the End of the World* (1948) was the first Japanese eyewitness account of the Hiroshima blast.

Boy O Boy
Under the scientific direction of Robert J Oppenheimer, the first atomic bomb was tested at Los Alamos in July 1945; it was called Trinity after the poem by John Donne. News of its success was quickly posted to allied leaders meeting in Potsdam.

Crazy Iris
A short story by the survivor, Masuji Ibuse, the title story of the 1985 collection edited by Kenzaburo Oē.

Eyes All The Way Down
For Dr. Hachiya's dream see *Hiroshima Diary*, pp101, 144: for the scientific 'eyeball' see Richard Rhodes, *The Making of the Atomic Bomb*, p67
'...the timeless inscription' refers to the words carved at the cenotaph: 'LET THE SOULS HERE REST IN PEACE FOR WE SHALL NOT REPEAT THIS EVIL'

Lines Found in My Father's Hiroshima Folder
My father, Neville Hill, an activist in the Australian Peace Movement and an organizer for the Amalgamated Engineering Union, went to several peace conferences in Japan in the seventies and eighties.

Listening Out

Burton Watson, the prolific translator of Japanese and Chinese classics, sailed into Japan in 1945 with the victorious US Navy. Following his post-war studies at Columbia, he has lived in Japan since 1960. He tells the story of the *uguisu*, Japan's celebrated bush warbler, in his essays, *The Rainbow World* (1990).

www.ingramcontent.com/pod-product-compliance
Lightning Source LLC
Chambersburg PA
CBHW031154160426
43193CB00008B/364